# IT'S TIME TO BAKE HOLIDAY GUMDROP COOKIES

# It's Time to Bake HOLIDAY GUMDROP COOKIES

## Walter the Educator

Silent King Books
A WhichHead Entertainment Imprint

Copyright © 2025 by Walter the Educator

All rights reserved. No part of this book may be reproduced in any manner whatsoever without written per- mission except in the case of brief quotations embodied in critical articles and reviews.

First Printing, 2025

Disclaimer

This book is a literary work; the story is not about specific persons, locations, situations, and/or circumstances unless mentioned in a historical context. Any resemblance to real persons, locations, situations, and/or circumstances is coincidental. This book is for entertainment and informational purposes only. The author and publisher offer this information without warranties expressed or implied. No matter the grounds, neither the author nor the publisher will be accountable for any losses, injuries, or other damages caused by the reader's use of this book. The use of this book acknowledges an understanding and acceptance of this disclaimer.

It's Time to Bake HOLIDAY GUMDROP COOKIES is a collectible early learning book by Walter the Educator suitable for all ages belonging to Walter the Educator's Time to Bake Book Series. Collect more books at WaltertheEducator.com

**USE THE EXTRA SPACE TO TAKE NOTES AND DOCUMENT YOUR MEMORIES**

# HOLIDAY GUMDROP COOKIES

The snowflakes fall, the wind does blow,

# It's Time to Bake Holiday Gumdrop Cookies

It's time for baking, let's go, let's go!

We'll gather our tools and start our quest,

Holiday cookies are simply the best!

Flour and sugar, a pinch of fun,

Measuring cups, oh, here's the big one!

Mixing bowls in red and green,

Holiday magic, a tasty scene.

Now crack the eggs, just one or two,

And stir them in, careful what you do!

A sprinkle of salt, a splash of cream,

This is turning into a cookie dream.

The butter melts and blends just right,

We stir and mix with all our might.

Now add the gumdrops, red and gold,

These chewy gems make cookies bold!

# It's Time to Bake
# Holiday Gumdrop Cookies

Roll the dough out, soft and sweet,

It's sticky and smells like a holiday treat.

With cookie cutters, we press and play,

Stars and hearts for a festive display.

Onto the tray, we line them up,

Rows of cookies soon to fill our cup.

The oven's warm, the timer is set,

Oh, what fun, we're not done yet!

As they bake, the house fills with cheer,

The scent of cookies is finally here.

We wait and watch, our patience grows,

Peeking through the oven, how cute, who knows?

Ding goes the timer! Out they come,

Golden and ready, oh, yum, yum, yum!

We'll let them cool before we taste,

# It's Time to Bake
# Holiday Gumdrop Cookies

A holiday treat we'd never waste.

Frosting and sprinkles, a colorful swirl,

Decorate cookies for every boy and girl.

Add some gumdrops on top for flair,

Holiday cookies made with care.

Now it's time to share our creation,

Spreading joy and sweet sensation.

With friends and family, near and far,

# It's Time to Bake
# Holiday Gumdrop Cookies

Holiday cookies are the best by far!

# ABOUT THE CREATOR

Walter the Educator is one of the pseudonyms for Walter Anderson. Formally educated in Chemistry, Business, and Education, he is an educator, an author, a diverse entrepreneur, and he is the son of a disabled war veteran. "Walter the Educator" shares his time between educating and creating. He holds interests and owns several creative projects that entertain, enlighten, enhance, and educate, hoping to inspire and motivate you. Follow, find new works, and stay up to date with Walter the Educator™

at WaltertheEducator.com

www.ingramcontent.com/pod-product-compliance
Lightning Source LLC
LaVergne TN
LVHW052010060526
838201LV00059B/3947